Varalaxmi Vratam

Illustrations: Sujata Saha

Publisher: DivineBharat

Varalaxmi vratam

ISBN Number : 978-93-343-3314-5

Illustrations: Sujata Saha

Publisher: DivineBharat

www.divinebharat.co

CONTENTS

1. Introduction
2. Items Required for the Pooja
3. Preparation & Setup
4. Pooja Procedure (Step-by-Step)
• Kalasha Sthapana
• Sankalpam (Taking the Vow)
• Ganapati Pujan
• Kalasha Pooja
• Varalaxmi Alankaram (Decorating the Goddess)
• Shodasha Upachara Puja (16 offering given with devotion to goddess)
• Anga Pooja
5. Lakshmi Ashtottara Shatanamavali
6. Final Pooja Offerings jncluding
7. [Thorabandhanam (Tying the Sacred
8. Thread), Vayana Daana (Offering to Married Women)]
9. Hindi Vrat katha
Sanskrit Vrat katha
10. Sri Ashta Lakshmi Strotram
11. Conclusion of Varalaxmi vratam
12. Punar Puja and Next Day Rituals

Introduction

Varalakshmi Vratham is a significant Hindu festival dedicated to **Goddess Varalaxmi**, a benevolent form of **Goddess Laxmi**, the consort of Lord Vishnu. The name *Varalaxmi* means *"the giver of boons"*.

Worshipping **Goddess Varalaxmi** is believed to be equivalent to worshipping the **Ashtalaxmi**, the eight divine forms of Lakshmi — **Adi Lakshmi** (spiritual wealth), **Dhana Lakshmi** (wealth), **Dhanya Lakshmi** (food and agriculture), **Gaja Lakshmi** (prosperity), **Santana Lakshmi** (offspring), **Dhairya Lakshmi** (courage), **Vijaya Lakshmi** (victory), and **Vidya Lakshmi** (knowledge). Thus, Varalakshmi embodies the blessings of all eight aspects of abundance and well-being. Worshipping her is believed to bring blessings of **wealth, health, prosperity**, and **family well-being**.

The **origin of Varalaxmi vratam** is found in the **Skanda Purana**, where **Lord Shiva** reveals its significance to **Goddess Parvati**. The vrat was first observed by a pious woman named **Charumati** in the city of **Kundina**, following a divine vision from

Goddess Lakshmi. Impressed by her devotion, the goddess blessed Charumati and her family with prosperity. Inspired by her example, many women began observing the vrat to seek the blessings of health, wealth, and happiness.

This vratham is traditionally observed on the **Friday before the full moon (Purnima)** in the **Hindu month of Shravan**. It is primarily celebrated in **South Indian states** like **Tamil Nadu, Karnataka, Andhra Pradesh, Telangana** and also in **Maharashtra and Odisha**.

Married women observe this fast and perform the pooja to pray for the longevity and prosperity of their husbands and families. **Unmarried women** and those desiring children may also perform the vrat for divine blessings. It is advised to take guidance from elders to follow the rituals correctly.

Items Required for the pooja

1. Idol & Setup

1. Face idol of Goddess Lakshmi or Ashtalakshmi (ready-made)
2. Wooden plank or **Peeta/ Thambaalam** (to place the idol)
3. **Kalash** (pot) filled with **raw rice** and **scented water** (cardamom, saffron, cloves, edible camphor, mace)
4. **Mango leaves** (to place in Kalash)
5. **Coconut** (with or without husk, for Kalash)
6. **New blouse piece** (to offer or drape on Goddess)
7. **Devi Vastra** (saree or cloth for the deity)
8. **Devi Abhushan** (jewelry/ornaments for the deity)
9. **Mirror** and **comb** (auspicious items for goddess decoration)

2. Sacred Threads: Thoram and Pongu Nool

10.Thoram: A sacred **thread** made of **nine strands, tied with nine knots,** and smeared with turmeric. It is tied on the right wrist by women after the pooja.

11.Pongu Nool: A **single turmeric-coated thread t**ied around the neck or hand. Married women wear both Thoram and Pongu Nool, while unmarried girls tie only the Thoram.

12. **Karimani Mala** *(Black bead chain worn by married women)*
A necklace made of tiny black beads, considered a symbol of marital status and protection from evil.

3. Pooja Essentials

13. **Turmeric powder**
14. **Kumkum**
15. **Sandal paste (Chandan)**
16. **Vibhuti** (sacred ash)
17. **Akshata** (turmeric-coated whole rice)
18. **Betel leaves**
19. **Betel nuts**
20. **Dry dates**
21. **Coins** (including ₹1 coin for Thamboolam)
22. **Unbroken rice**
23. **Small puja bell**

4. Offerings (Naivedyam & Others)

24. **Panchamrit** (milk, curd, honey, ghee, sugar/jaggery,)
25. **Naivedyam** – Traditional sweets like **Payasam, Appam, Boorelu**
26. **Fruits** (all seasonal varieties)
27. **Banana**
28. **Dry fruits & nuts**
29. **Curd**, **milk**, and **water**

30. **Prasad** (offered food)
31. **Banana saplings or leaves** (for pooja mandap decoration)

5. Puja Accessories
32. **Incense sticks (Agarbatti)**
33. **Ghee/oil lamp**
34. **Camphor** (for aarti)
35. **Sambrani** (resin incense for fumigation)
36. **Small oil lamp**
37. **Flower garlands**
38. **Fresh flowers**
39. **Lotus flower** (if available)

6. Decoration & Distribution
40. **Rangoli materials** – Rice flour and natural colors
41. **Thamboolam** *(A return gift set offered to* married *women after the pooja)* It usually includes **betel leaves**, **betel nuts**, **banana**, **coconut**, **turmeric thread**, **kumkum**, **blouse piece**, and a coin—symbolizing blessings and goodwill. Betel nuts, Turmeric-smeared thread -**Thoram**, Blouse piece, ₹1 coin
42. **Paper plates and bowls** (for distributing prasadam)

7. Miscellaneous
43. **Varalaxmi vratam Book**

Preparation & Setup

A. Preparations (Day Before the Vratam - Thursday)

The preparations for Varalakshmi Vratham traditionally begin a day prior, on Thursday . This day is dedicated to gathering all the required pooja items, cleaning the house, and setting up the altar.

1. **House Cleaning**: Clean the house thoroughly, especially the pooja space.
2. **Kolam (Rangoli)**: Decorate the pooja area with beautiful kolam or muggu using rice flour and natural colors.
3. **Peeta Setup**: Place a decorated wooden plank (**peeta** or **thambaalam**) where the Kalasha and Goddess Lakshmi will be installed.

B. Kalasha Preparation (On Vratham Day - Friday)

The **Kalasha** is the symbolic representation of Goddess Varalakshmi and is the central part of the pooja.

Steps to Prepare the Kalasha:

1. Select a clean pot, preferably made of silver, bronze, or brass.

2. Fill it up to the brim with scented water (water infused with cardamom, saffron, cloves, edible camphor, and Mace / Javitri)
or as per regional tradition,
fill it with raw rice, a lemon, coins, black beads (Karimani mala), turmeric sticks, dry fruits, and betel nuts.
3. Draw a swastika symbol on the Kalasha using turmeric or sandal paste.
4. Place 5 or 9 mango leaves in the mouth of the Kalasha.
5. Decorate a coconut with turmeric and kumkum; place it atop the Kalasha with pointed side upward.
6. Fix the face of Goddess Lakshmi or an image onto the coconut, symbolizing the deity.
7. Wrap a new blouse piece or a decorative cloth around the coconut of the Kalasha.
8. Place the Kalasha on a mound of raw rice on the wooden plank, facing **east**.

C. Decoration and Floral Arrangement

1. **Decorate the altar** with fresh **flowers and garlands**
2. Place banana saplings/ leaves on both sides of altar.
3. Place items such as **betel leaves, nuts, bananas, turmeric sticks**, **fruits**, **sweets** around the altar.

D. Thamboolam sets

Before the pooja, keep the following ready in a plate:

- Thoram and Pongu Nool
- 9 betel leaves
- 9 betel nuts
- 9 bananas
- 9 dates
- 9 turmeric sticks
- Kumkum box
- Black beads chain (**Karimani mala**)

These items are offered as part of the ritual and also prepared for distributing in **Thamboolam sets** to ladies after pooja .

E. After the Pooja

1. **Water in Kalasha**: The water should be respectfully offered to **plants rooted in the ground** (not potted). Avoid letting the water spill or flow in walkways.
2. **Coconut atop Kalasha**: Break it the next day and use it to prepare a sweet dish like **sweet Pongal**, **Modak**, or **Kozhukattai**.

Puja procedure

1. **Kalasha Sthapana**
Installation of the sacred pot representing Goddess Varalakshmi.

2. **Sankalpam** *(Vow Statement)*
Clasp the right palm over the left palm holding a flower, akshata, and place them on the right thigh.Chant:

Evamguna viseshana visistayamasyam shubha thithou, asmakam saha kutumbanam kshema sthairya vijaya ayur arogya aishwarya abhivr idhyartham, dharmartha kaama moksha chaturvidha purushartha siddhyartham,

ishta kamarthya siddhyartham, sathsanthana soubhaya shubha phalavapyartham varshe varshe prayuktham varalakshmi muddhishya varalakshmi preethyartham bhavishyottara purana kalpoktha prakarena yavaschakti dhyanavahanadhi shodashopachara pujan karishya.

Thadan gathwena kalasha pujan karishya.

Ganapati Pujan (Haridra Ganapati)

Make a cone shaped turmeric Ganesha (Haridra Ganapathi)
by mixing turmeric powder and few drops of water. Visualise Lord Ganesha and Place on left side of kalasha slightly forward.
Chant Ganesha sloka.

Suklam Bharadharam Vishnum
Sashivarnam Chaturbhujam
Prasanna vadanam dhyayeth
Sarvavighnopashantaye

Offer turmeric, flowers, akshata to Lord Ganesha seeking blessings.

Kalasha Pooja (Worship of the Sacred Pot)

In the Varalakshmi Vratham, the **Kalasha** represents **Goddess Varalakshmi** herself. Once **Ganapati Pooja** is completed, the **Kalasha is worshipped** as the divine seat of the goddess.
Offerings to Kalasha:

- Sprinkle **akshata** (turmeric-coated rice)
- Offer **flowers**, **haldi**, **kumkum**, and **sandal paste**
- Light **deepam** (lamp) and **agarbatti**

Chant the Kalasha Mantra:

Kalashasya mukhe Vishnu
Kante rudra samasritha
Moole thathra sthitho brahma
Madhye mathru ganaa smrutha
Kukshouthu sagara ssarve
Sapta dweepa vasundhara
Rugvedoda yajurveda
Samavedoh atharvana
Angaischa sahita ssarve
Kalashambu samasritha
Ayanthu lakshmi pujartham
Durithakshaya karaka

Next, chant the River Invocation Mantra:

Gangecha yamune chaiva
Godavari saraswati
Narmade sindhu kaveri
jalesmin sannidhim kuru

Evam kalasha puja

Varalakshmi Puja begins now:

Padmasane padmakare
sarvalokaika pujithe,
Narayana priye devi
supreetha bhava sarvada.

Varalaxmi Alankaram (Decorating the Goddess)

.The Kalasha now represents **Maa Varalakshmi**. Begin to decorate Her beautifully.

- **Blouse Piece / Saree Drape**:

Wrap a new **blouse piece or small saree cloth** around the neck of the Kalasha or around the coconut like a shawl. This is the vastram (garment) of the Goddess.

- **Face of Goddess Lakshmi (Optional)**:

If you have a **Varalakshmi face mask**, gently place or attach it to the coconut on the Kalasha.

If not, you can draw eyes with turmeric and kumkum or simply decorate the coconut as Her symbolic form.

- **Jewelry and Ornaments**:

Adorn the Kalasha with:

- **Chains or gold-plated jewelry**
- **Kumkum and turmeric dots**
- **Flower garlands (mala)** around the neck
- **Nose ring, earrings, bangles** (if available in doll-size)
- A small **mukut** (crown) or decorative headpiece
- **Decorate with Flowers**:

Place **fresh flowers** like jasmine,

marigold, or roses all around the Kalasha and pooja area. You may place flowers in the Goddess's "hair" if using a mask.

- **Place the Kalasha on a decorated Peeta (Wooden Plank)**:

Set the dressed Kalasha on a wooden plank (peeta or thambaalam) covered with a decorative cloth or banana leaf and **rangoli**.

Symbolic Representation

This beautifully adorned Kalasha is now **Varalaxmi Devi**. All further pooja, mantras, offerings, and aarti will be performed to Her in this form.

VARALAXMI
VRATAM
VASTRAM

Shodasha Upachara Puja

1.Dhyanam (Invocation)

Visualise the Goddess and pray to her by chanting this mantram

**Ksheerodarnava sambhuthe kamala kamalalaye,
Susthirabhava may gehe surasura namaskruthe
Sri Varalakshmi devatham dhyayami
Avahanam**

Visualise Goddess Varalakshmi in mind and offer flower or Akshatha to Kalasha or. Thereby we invoke the Goddess in the idol or image.

**Sarvamangala mangalye Vishnu vaksha sthalalaye,
Avahayami devee thwaam supreetha bhava sarvada,
Varalakshmi devatham avahayami**

2.Aasanam (offering seat)

Offer flowers at the feet and chant

Suryayutha nibha spoorthe sphura drathna vibhushitham,
Simhasana midham devee stheeyatham sura pujithe,
Rathna simhasanam samarpayami

3.Arghyam (washing hands)

Offer one spoon of water from the glass with water to the empty cup. Chant

Shuddodakam cha pathrastham gandha pushpadhi mishritham,
Arghyam dasyami the devee gruhaana sura pujithe,
Arghyam samarpayami

4.Paadhyam (washing the feet)

Suvasitha jalam ramya sarva theertha samudbhavam,
Paadhyam gruhaana thwam sarvadeva namaskruthe,
Paadhyam samarpayami

5.Aachamanam (Inner Purification)

Offer one spoon of water from the cup with water to empty cup and chant

Suvarna kalashaa neetham chandanagaru samyutham,
Gruhaana achamanam devee mayaa dattham shubhapradhe,
Aachamaneeyam samarpayami

6.Panchamrutha Snanam (offering bath with Panchamrita)

Offer bath with few drops or a spoon of panchamritham to the Goddess by chanting the below sloka

Payodadhi gruthopetham sharkaramadhu samyutham,
Panchamrutha snanamidham gruhaana kamalalaye,
Panchamrutha snanam samarpayami
Shuddodaka Snanam

Offer bath with few drops or a spoon of water to the Goddess by chanting the below sloka

Gangajalam mayaaneetham mahadeva shirasthitham,
Shuddodaka snanamidham gruhaana vidhu sodhari,
Shuddodaka snanam samarpayami

7.Vasthra yugmam (offering dress)

Offer a Gejje Vastra (cotton thread made of cotton, haldi, kumkum & chandan paste) by chanting the below slokam

Surarchitanghri yugale dukoola vasana priye,
Vasthrayugmam pradasyami gruhaana hari vallabhe,
Vasthra yugmam samarpayami

8.Abharanam (offering jewelry)

Offer any jewelry or akshata chanting
Keyura kankane divye haaranupura mekhala,
Vibhushananya moolyani gruhaana rushi pujithe,

Abharanani samaryami

9.Upavitham (Yagnopaveetham- sacred thread)

Offer another Gejje Vastra to the Goddess by chanting

Thaptha hema krutham suthram muktadama vibhushitham
Upavitha midham devi gruhaana thwam shubhapradhe,
Upavitham samarpayami

10.Gandham (offering sandal-paste)

Offer gandham (chandanam paste) to the Goddess

Karpuragaru kasturi rochanadhi bhiranvitham, Gandham dasyamyaham devee prithyartham prathigruhyatham, Gandham samarpayami

11.Akshatha (Offering consecrated rice)

Offer akshatha to the Goddess

Akshatha dhavala devi shaliyam sthadula shubha,
Haridra kumkumopetha gruhyathaa mabdhi puthrike,
Akshatha samarpayami

12.Pushpa Puja (offering flowers)

Offer flowers to the Goddess by chanting this slokam.

Mallika jaaji kusumai champakairva kulaisthatha,
Shathapathrai scha kalharai pujayami haripriye,
Pushpai pujayami

Anga Puja (Worship of the Divine Form)

(Offer a flower or akshata at each step)

1. **Chanchalayai namaha — Padhau pujayami**
(I worship Her feet)
2. **Chapalayai namaha — Januni pujayami**
(I worship Her knees)
3. **Peethambara dharayai namaha — Ooroo pujayami**
(I worship Her thighs)
4. **Kamala vasinyai namaha — Katim pujayami**
(I worship Her waist)
5. **Padmalayayai namaha — Naabhim pujayami**
(I worship Her navel)
6. **Madanamatre namaha — Sthanau pujayami**
(I worship Her bosom/chest)
7. **Lalithayai namaha — Bhujadwayam pujayami**
(I worship Her two arms)
8. **Kambh kantyai namaha — Kantam pujayami**
(I worship Her neck)
9. **Sumukhayai namaha — Mukham pujayami**
(I worship Her face)

10. **Shreeyai namaha — Oshtau pujayami**
(I worship Her lips)
11. **Sunasikayai namaha — Nasikam pujayami**
(I worship Her nose)
12. **Sunetrai namaha — Netram pujayami**
(I worship Her eyes)
13. **Ramayai namaha — Karnau pujayami**
(I worship Her ears)
14. **Kamalayai namaha — Shirah pujayami**
(I worship Her head)
15. **Varalakshmyai namaha — Sarvaangani pujayami**
(I worship Her entire form)

Lakshmi Ashtottara Shatanamavali

(108 Names of Goddess Lakshmi)

Om prakrityai namah .
Om vikrityai namah .
Om vidyaayai namah .
Om sarvabhuutahitapradaayai namah .
Om shraddhaayai namah .
Om vibhuutyai namah .
Om surabhyai namah .
Om paramaatmikaayai namah .
Om vaache namah .
Om padmaalayaayai namah .
Om padmaayai namah .
Om shuchaye namah .
Om svaahaayai namah .
Om svadhaayai namah .
Om sudhaayai namah .
Om dhanyaayai namah .
Om hiranmayyai namah .
Om laxmyai namah .
Om nityapushhtaayai namah .
Om vibhaavaryai namah .
Om adityai namah .
Om ditye namah .
Om diipaayai namah .
Om vasudhaayai namah .
Om vasudhaarinyai namah .
Om kamalaayai namah .
Om kaantaayai namah .

Om kaamaaxyai namah .
Om krodhasambhavaayai namah .
Om anugrahapradaayai namah .
Om buddhaye namah .
Om anaghaayai namah .
Om harivallabhaayai namah .
Om ashokaayai namah .
Om amritaayai namah .
Om diiptaayai namah .
Om lokashokavinaashinyai namah .
Om dharmanilayaayai namah .
Om karunaayai namah .
Om lokamaatre namah .
Om padmapriyaayai namah .
Om padmahastaayai namah .
Om padmaaxyai namah .
Om padmasundaryai namah .
Om padmodbhavaayai namah .
Om padmamukhyai namah .
Om padmanaabhapriyaayai namah .
Om ramaayai namah .
Om padmamaalaadharaayai namah .
Om devyai namah .
Om padminyai namah .
Om padmagandhinyai namah .
Om punyagandhaayai namah .
Om suprasannaayai namah .
Om prasaadaabhimukhyai namah .
Om prabhaayai namah .
Om chandravadanaayai namah .
Om chandraayai namah .

Om chandrasahodaryai namah .
Om chaturbhujaayai namah .
Om chandraruupaayai namah .
Om indiraayai namah .
Om indushiitalaayai namah .
Om aahlaadajananyai namah .
Om pushhtayai namah .
Om shivaayai namah .
Om shivakaryai namah .
Om satyai namah .
Om vimalaayai namah .
Om vishvajananyai namah .
Om tushhtayai namah .
Om daaridryanaashinyai namah .
Om priitipushhkarinyai namah .
Om shaantaayai namah .
Om shuklamaalyaambaraayai namah .
Om shriyai namah .
Om bhaaskaryai namah .
Om bilvanilayaayai namah .
Om varaarohaayai namah .
Om yashasvinyai namah .
Om vasundharaayai namah .
Om udaaraa.ngaayai namah .
Om harinyai namah .
Om hemamaalinyai namah .
Om dhanadhaanyakarye namah .
Om siddhaye namah .
Om strainasaumyaayai namah .
Om shubhapradaaye namah .
Om nripaveshmagataanandaayai namah .

Om varalaxmyai namah .
Om vasupradaayai namah .
Om shubhaayai namah .
Om hiranyapraakaaraayai namah .
Om samudratanayaayai namah .
Om jayaayai namah .
Om mangalaa devyai namah .
Om vishhnuvaxassthalasthitaayai namah .
Om vishhnupatnyai namah .
Om prasannaaxyai namah .
Om naaraayanasamaashritaayai namah .
Om daaridryadhv.nsinyai namah .
Om devyai namah .
Om sarvopadrava vaarinyai namah .
Om navadurgaayai namah .
Om mahaakaalyai namah .
Om brahmaavishhnushivaatmikaayai namah .
Om trikaalagyaanasampannaayai namah .
Om bhuvaneshvaryai namah .

Om Ashottara shatanama pujam samarpayami

Final Pooja Offerings

1. **Dhoopam (Offering Incense)**

Offer incense sticks (agarbatti) to the Goddess while chanting

Dashangam guggulopetam sugandham cha manoharam
Dhoopam dadhyami deveshi varalakshmi grihana tam
Dhoopam samarpayami

2. Deepam (Offering Lamp)

Light the ghee or oil lamp and offer it to the Goddess with the following mantra:

Ghrutaktavarti samyuktam andhakaram vinashakam
Deepam dadhyami te devi grihana mudita bhava
Deepam samarpayami

3. Naivedyam (Offering Food)

Offer prepared naivedyam (sweets, fruits, coconut) to the Goddess.

Naivedyam shatrasopetam dadhi madhu ajya samyutam
Nana bhakshya phalopetam grihana harivallabhe
Naivedyam samarpayami

Also offer **paaneeyam (drinking water)**:

Ghanasara sugandhena mishritam pushpasitakam
Paaneeyam grihyatam devi sheetalam sumanoharam
Paaneeyam samarpayami

4. **Thamboolam** (**Offering Betel Leaves & Nuts)**
Offer betel leaves, nuts, dry dates, and coins.

Poogephala samayuktam nagavalli dalairyutam
Karpura churna samyuktam thamboolam pratigruhyatam
Thamboolam samarpayami

5. Neerajanam (Offering Aarti with Camphor)
Offer camphor-lit aarti to the Goddess.

Neerajanam samaneetam karpurena samanvitam
Tubhyam dadhyami aham devi grihyatam vishnu vallabhe

Neerajanam samarpayami

6. Mantra Pushpam (Offering Sacred Mantra Flower)
Offer akshata or flowers at Her feet while chanting:

Padmasane padmakare sarva lokaika pujite
Narayana priye devi supreeto bhava sarvada
Mantra pushpam samarpayami

7. Pradakshina (Circumambulations)
Perform **5 self-circumambulations (pradakshina)** around the pooja space.

Yani kani cha papani janmantar kritani cha
Tani tani pranashyanti pradakshina pade pade

8. Namaskaram (Offering Final Salutations)
Offer your full prostrations and prayer:

Samasta loka janani namaste vishnu vallabhe
Pahimam bhakta varade varalakshmi namo namah
Sri Varalakshmi devataayi namaskaran samarpayami

9. Atha Thoragranthi Pooja (Worship of the Sacred Thread)

Worship the turmeric-smeared nine-knotted thread (**Thoram**) by offering sandal paste, turmeric, kumkum, flowers, and akshata.

Granthi Mantras (For each knot):

Kamalayai namah – Prathama granthim pujayami
Ramayai namah – Dviteeya granthim pujayami
Lokamatre namah – Truteeya granthim pujayami
Vishvajananyai namah – Chaturtha granthim pujayami
Mahalakshmyai namah – Panchama granthim pujayami
Ksheerabhi tanayayai namah – Sashtama granthim pujayami
Vishvasakshinyai namah – Saptama granthim pujayami
Chandrasodaryai namah – Ashtama granthim pujayami
Harivallabhyai namah – Navama granthim pujayami

10. Thorabandhanam (Tying the Sacred Thread)

Tie the sacred **Thoram** on the **right wrist**, while chanting:

Badhnami dakshine haste nava sutram shubhapradam
Putrapoutra abhivriddhishcha saubhagyam dehi me rame

11. Vayana Vidhi (Offering Sacred Food to the Goddess)

Offer **Vayanam** (usually 12 small poori or sweet offerings) to the Goddess:

Evam sampujya kalyanim varalakshmim swa shaktitah
Daathavyam dwadasha poopam vayanam hi dvijatayeh

12. Vayana Daana (Offering to Married Women)

Distribute **vayanam** (along with thamboolam) to other **Sumangalis (married women)** by chanting:

Indira pratigrihnatu Indira vai dadati cha
Indira tarako bhabhyam Indirayai namo namah

Iti Varalakshmi Vrata Pooja Vidhanam Sampurnam

Hindi Vrat katha

Charumathi, a Brahmin woman lived in a town, Kundina. She was very humble and kind in her nature. She was very much devoted to her husband and family.

One night, Goddess Laxmi appeared in her dream and told her to worship Vara Laxmi and seek her blessings. Goddess Laxmi also explained the Vrata procedure and the best day to observe Vara Laxmi Vrata. Laxmi asked Charumathi to observe Varalaxmi Vrataon the Friday just before Shravan Purnima, the Full Moon day in Shravan Month.

Charumathi informed about the dream to his husband and family. She also told to her friends and the word spread throughout the town. On the Friday before Shravan Purnima, Charumathi along with her family, friends and the women of the town observe Vara Laxmi Vrata. They worshipped Vara Laxmi with utmost devotion and offered special recipes and fruits to please her. Goddess Vara Laxmi appeared before them and granted boons to all of them. Their houses were filled with grains, diamonds, jewels and gold. They all lived happily in their rest of life. Since the time, women have begun observing Vara Laxmi Vrata every year on the specific Friday.

nyavedayat. Tatah Varalakshmi devi taasam puratah prakatya sarvaabhyah varaan dattavati. Tesham grihaani dhaanya ratna mani hiranyamayaaani abhavan. Taah sarvaah sukhena chiraaya jeevitavatyaah. Tasmaatkaalaat striyah prativarsham tasmineva shukravaasare Varalakshmi vratamaacharanti.

Sanskrit Vrat katha

Charumati nama braahmani kundinaakhye nagare vasati sma. Saa swabhaavatah ateeva vinayee karunaasheela cha aasit. Saa swaptye kutumbe cha atyadhikam bhaktimati aasit. Ekadaa ratrau Lakshmidevi swapne tasyai drishtvaa vratam aakhyatavati Varalakshmim poojayitvaa tasyaah kripaam praarthaya. Devi Lakshmi Varalakshmi vratavidhi cha uttamam dinam cha tasyai uktavati. Shraavanapurnimaapoorva shukravaasare Varalakshmi vratam kartavyamiti devi uktavati. Charumati swapnavrittaantam patye kutumbe cha niveditavati. Saa swamitrebhyah api uktavati, nagaramadhye vaakyam prasaaritam. Tasmineva shukravaasare Charumati svakutumba mitrastribhih saha Varalakshmi vratam kritavati. Saa ateeva bhaktyaa devim poojayitvaa visheshapaakaannaani phalaani cha nyavedayat. Tatah Varalakshmi devi taasam puratah prakatya sarvaabhyah varaan dattavati. Tesham grihaani dhaanya ratna mani hiranyamayaaani abhavan. Taah sarvaah sukhena chiraaya jeevitavatyaah. Tasmaatkaalaat striyah prativarsham tasmineva shukravaasare Varalakshmi vratamaacharanti.

Sri Ashtalaxmi Lakshmi Strotram

Adilakshmi

Sumanasavandita sundari maadhavi,
chandra sahodari hemamaye
Muniganamandita mokshapradayini,
manjulabhashini vedanute
Pankajavaasini devasupoopita,
sadgunavarshini shaantiyute
Jayajaya he madhusudana kaamini,
Adilakshmi sada paalaya maam 1

Dhanyalakshmi

Ahikali kalmashanaashini kaamini,
vaidikarupini vedamaye
Ksheerasamudbhava mangalarupini,
mantranivaasini mantranute
Mangaladaayini ambujavaasini,
devaganaashrita paadayute
Jayajaya he madhusudana kaamini,
Dhanyalakshmi sada paalaya maam 2

Dhairyalakshmi

Jayavaravarnini vaishnavi bhaargavi,
mantrasvarupini mantramaye
Suraganapoojita shighraphalaprada,
jnanavikaasini shaastranute
Bhavabhayahaarini paapavimochani,
saadhujanaashrita paadayute
Jayajaya he madhusudana kaamini,
Dhairyalakshmi sada paalaya maam 3

Gajalakshmi

Jayajaya durgatinashini kaamini,
sarvaphalaprada shaastramaye
Rathagaja turagapadaadi samaavrita,
parijanamandita lokanute
Harihara brahma supoojita sevita,
taapanivaarini paadayute
Jayajaya he madhusudana kaamini,
Gajalakshmi rupena paalaya maam 4

Santanalakshmi

Ahikhaga vaahini mohini chakrini,
raagavivardhini jnanamaye
Gunaganavaaridhi lokahitaishini,
svarasapta bhooshita gaananute
Sakala suraasura devamunishwara,
maanavavandita paadayute
Jayajaya he madhusudana kaamini,
Santanalakshmi tvam paalaya maam 5

Vijayalakshmi

Jaya kamalaasani sadgatidaayini,
jnanavikaasini gaanamaye
Anudinamarchita kunkumadhoosara
bhooshita vaasita vaadyanute
Kanakadharaastuti vaibhava vandita,
shankara deshika maanya pade
Jayajaya he madhusudana kaamini,
Vijayalakshmi sada paalaya maam 6

Vidyalakshmi

Pranata sureshwari bhaarati bhaargavi,
shokavinaashini ratnamaye
Manimayabhooshita karnavibhooshana,
shaantisamaavrita haasyamukhe
Navanidhidaayini kalimalahaarini, kaamita
phalaprada hastayute
Jayajaya he madhusudana kaamini,
Vidyalakshmi sada paalaya maam 7

Dhanalakshmi

Dhimidhimi dhindhimi dhindhimi
dhindhimi, dundubhi naada supoornamaye
Ghumaghum ghunghum ghunghum
ghunghum, shankhaninaada suvaadyanute
Vedapuraanetihaasa supoojita,
vaidikamarga pradarshayute
Jayajaya he madhusudana kaamini,
Dhanalakshmi rupena paalaya maam 8

Conclusion of Varalaxmi vratam

After listening to the **Varalaxmi vratam Katha**, it is customary to gently **sprinkle akshata** (turmeric-coated sacred rice) on one's head as a symbol of divine blessings.

Then, **thamboolam** — consisting of **betel leaves, areca nut, a coin, and turmeric-kumkum** — is respectfully offered to **married women (Sumangalis)** as part of the sacred sharing.

All devotees should then **partake of the prasadam**, which includes the food items offered to the Goddess during the puja.

Those who perform the vrat should ideally **observe a simple fast that night** and continue to **pray with sincerity and devotion.**

Punar Puja and Next Day Rituals

On the **next morning**, usually , a brief ritual called **Punar Puja** (concluding worship) is performed to formally mark the **end of the Varalaxmi vratam.** After offering prayers, **Goddess Lakshmi's image or Kalasham** is respectfully lifted from the puja place and safely stored for use in the **next year's Varalakshmi Puja**.

The **coconut placed atop the Kalasham** should be **broken** and used to prepare a sweet dish like **Modak, Pongal, or Kozhukattai**. The **water from the Kalasham** should be **poured to plants**, preferably sacred or flowering ones like **Tulsi**, ensuring that the water does **not flow onto walkways or get stepped on**.

All **biodegradable offerings** such as **flowers, turmeric, kumkum**, and other organic materials used in the puja should be respectfully **disposed of in a well or clean flowing water** — again, ensuring it is a **place not frequently stepped on by people**.These actions complete the vratam with sanctity and devotion, maintaining both **spiritual and environmental purity**.

9 789334 333145

Printed at Repro India Ltd.